Wedding Planning for the Bride-to-Be

Your Guide to an Organized and Memorable Wedding

April Hall

This book is dedicated to newly engaged brides-to-be. Congratulations! Use this book to plan your perfect wedding as easy and stress free as possible.

Copyright Act of 1976, the scanning, uploading and electronic sharing of any part of this book without the explicit written consent or permission of the publisher constitutes unlawful piracy and the theft of intellectual property.

If you would like to use material or content from this book (other than for review purposes), prior written permission must be obtained from the publisher.

You can contact the publishing company at admin@speedypublishing.com. Thank you for not infringing on the author's rights.

Speedy Publishing LLC (c) 2014
40 E. Main St., #1156
Newark, DE 19711
www.speedypublishing.co

Ordering Information:
Quantity sales; Special discounts are available on quantity purchases by corporations, associations, and others. For details, contact the "Special Sales Department" at the address above.

This is a reprint book.

Manufactured in the United States of America

Table of Contents

Publisher's Notes i

Chapter 1: Introduction 1

Chapter 2: Planning the Perfect Wedding 2

Chapter 3: The Advantages of a Wedding Planner 5

Chapter 4: Wedding Expenses and Your Budget 8

Chapter 5: Choosing Your Wedding Party? 11

Chapter 6: The Guest List 14

Chapter 7: Choosing the Perfect Location for Your Wedding and Reception 17

Chapter 8: Planning Your Wedding Reception 20

Chapter 9: Organizing the Wedding Ceremony 23

Chapter 10: Choosing Your Wedding Music 26

Chapter 11: Selecting Wedding Invitations 29

Chapter 12: Choosing Flowers for Your Wedding Day 32

Chapter 13: Your Wedding Pictures – Hire A Professional 35

Chapter 14: Wedding Cake Options 38

Chapter 15: Wedding Toasts and Etiquette 41

Chapter 16: Choosing Your Honeymoon Destination 44

Chapter 17: Wedding To-Do List 47

MEET THE AUTHOR 49

Publisher's Notes

Disclaimer

This publication is intended to provide helpful and informative material. It is not intended to diagnose, treat, cure, or prevent any health problem or condition, nor is intended to replace the advice of a physician. No action should be taken solely on the contents of this book. Always consult your physician or qualified health-care professional on any matters regarding your health and before adopting any suggestions in this book or drawing inferences from it.

The author and publisher specifically disclaim all responsibility for any liability, loss or risk, personal or otherwise, which is incurred as a consequence, directly or indirectly, from the use or application of any contents of this book.

Any and all product names referenced within this book are the trademarks of their respective owners. None of these owners have sponsored, authorized, endorsed, or approved this book.

Always read all information provided by the manufacturers' product labels before using their products. The author and publisher are not responsible for claims made by manufacturers.

Chapter 1: Introduction

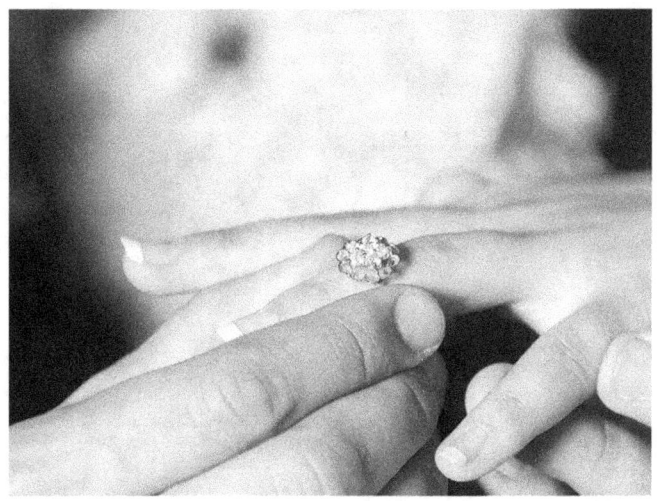

Thank you for downloading my Wedding book. Planning and organizing a wedding is a huge event and one that can become overwhelming without some guidance and help.

Getting engaged is a wonderful and exhilarating time. It's after the tears of joy have subsided, that the reality of planning your wedding day hits home. Planning and executing a smooth wedding can be a stressful thing for both the future bride and groom.

Use this wedding guide to assist with your planning and the details to ensure you have a memorable and wonderful wedding day.

Chapter 2: Planning the Perfect Wedding

A wedding can be a monumental task for anyone, especially if you have never planned a wedding before. There are many important tasks that must be completed, and all of these take time; this is essentially, what the engagement period involves.

The average engagement period in the United States is sixteen months. For you to make the best use of this time, you need to spread out all of the required actions in an orderly fashion. This way you won't feel rushed and you can make the best decisions for each action as required.

From the beginning of your engagement period to about nine months before the intended wedding date, you need to start a wedding folder or binder. All interesting ideas that you come across regarding bridal gowns and fashion ideas, lifestyle ideas, design, and food should be placed in this folder or binder.

This includes checking out online sources, printing them out, and placing them in the folder on your desktop. It doesn't hurt to have a notepad with you as well. This way you can jot down notes and ideas as they come to you.

You need to determine exactly how much you have to spend. This includes the amount of money you and your fiancé have to spend, as well as any money that your families are contributing to the wedding. You should also start to think about who you want to be in your wedding party.

In addition, you need to start the guest list of who will attend your wedding. This list should include contact information, gifts, RSVPs, and any other relevant information that you feel you need. It's important to get as accurate a head count early on so that you can more accurately predict how much your wedding will cost based on food, hall reservations, etc.

At this point, you should also determine whether you will hire a wedding planner or not. You should also research caterers, bands, florists, and photographers.

By the eight-month mark to your wedding date, you should have hired the photographer and videographer. You don't have to talk yet about how the pictures should be taken, but you should know if the photographer and videographer are available for that date and reserve them. Additionally, evaluate the gigs of potential acts to see how they do in front of audiences, then reserve the act you like best.

You should have picked out a dress by this time, as you should schedule at least three fitting sessions to ensure that the dress fits well come wedding day. You should register at a minimum of three retailers. This is also the perfect time to launch a wedding website; you don't have to spend money for this – you can launch it on a site such as weddingchannel.com. Put the date of the wedding, the travel information, and the accommodations on this page, then send out the link to invitees.

As you get closer to the wedding day, six months and sooner, you need to have more specific details in place and finalize arrangements regarding necessities (such as portable toilets for outdoor wedding), the florist, and transportation needs.

You also need to begin constructing a day-of timeline involving events such as the cutting of the cake and the first dance. You need to follow up on such important items as the wedding invitations, ordering the cake, booking the rehearsal-dinner venues, choosing the hair and makeup artists, and finalizing the music.

Essentially, you need to have a good plan of all the items that must be taken care of in order to have a successful wedding that is as stress-free as possible. Keep in mind that professionals such as wedding planners, photographers, videographers, and music acts can be booked months in advance. So you can't wait until the last minute (i.e. even six months ahead of time is often considered "last minute" in these cases) to book them.

Know the items that can be delayed until later and get back to those at a later time, while you take care of the items that need to be handled more promptly. By having a good plan of everything that needs to be done and setting up a timeline of when these things need to be completed, you can have the wedding of your dreams without stressing out too much in putting it together.

Chapter 3: The Advantages of a Wedding Planner

After the excitement of becoming engaged wears off, your next consideration is to start planning your wedding. You may be wondering if you should be handling all of the details yourself when it comes to organizing and planning your wedding. Or should you employ a wedding planner to handle all or some of it. We will consider both options below.

In today's difficult economic climate, many engaged couples want to save as much money on their wedding as possible. Couples spent an average of $30,000 on their weddings in 2013, no small amount of money, especially for the couple that is about to embark on their new life together.

The first instinct of those who want to save money is to not hire a wedding planner. This can help save some money, as wedding planners can cost anywhere from $250 to $15,000, depending upon how involved they are in the planning process of your wedding. Additionally, the bride (and groom) can have much more hands-on experience in designing and planning their wedding themselves than if they allow a wedding planner to handle the majority of it.

Nowadays, with the resources available on the Internet, a bride-to-be can more easily assemble everything that is needed for a great wedding without having to trek all over town to find the right suppliers and professionals. Instead, she can surf the Internet to find the resources and professionals she needs. With the advent of the mobile Web, she can do the necessary research even on-the-go via her tablet or Smartphone, thus making it easier for today's prospective brides to formulate a wedding than in generations past.

However, before you totally dismiss hiring a wedding planner based on costs, consider the following. Wedding planners often know of resources and have connections that can help you save money when you're getting the right dress, booking the proper venues, hiring the caterer, the music group, and the videographer, etc. As a result, you'll often pay less than you would if you were doing the detailed work yourself. Overall, the cost of hiring a wedding planner will often pay for itself in many cases.

Also, consider if you don't have much time on your hands. If you are involved in a very busy career that requires a lot of hands-on work, you may be better served to leave most of the details to the wedding planner. A wedding planner knows where to go and can get the best values, so they can complete the preparations much more quickly and with much less stress than you can.

Having less stress during your engagement can keep the romanticism at an all-time high so that you can more thoroughly enjoy this period in your life. Any problems that crop up will be dealt with by the wedding planner, often with little to no interaction required from the bride. Thus, weigh the cost of hiring a wedding planner versus having to deal with the stress and anxiety of planning out every detail for yourself.

Hiring a wedding planner will add extra cost to your wedding. However, it can also pay for itself in terms of discounts gained when booking venues and professionals, as well as reducing the amount of stress and anxiety felt during the planning process.

There is no one right answer; every engaged couple will be different. It's best to analyze exactly what you want in your wedding and how much time you have to devote to it. Then you can see if the benefits of hiring a wedding planner will outweigh the costs.

Chapter 4: Wedding Expenses and Your Budget

While you are excited about your upcoming wedding you need to be aware that the next several months will be exhilarating but busy. You want to set time aside for careful planning to ensure that your wedding is stress free and memorable.

To do this, you need to carefully consider exactly what will take place during your wedding and how many people will be there. This will give you an approximation of how much it will cost and what you'll have to do to make it happen. We will explore this in greater detail below.

First, you need to decide approximately how many people are going to be at your wedding and at your wedding reception. This will give you a good idea of what types of venues will be suitable for your wedding and for the reception.

You also need to take into consideration the theme of your wedding. Do you want a traditional, in-church wedding, a wedding on the beach, a wedding up in the mountains, etc.? This, too, will help you to narrow down the perfect venues for your wedding and reception.

When it comes to the actual ceremony, you should consider such expenses as the marriage license, officiates fee, the location fee, the ring pillows, and the musician's fees. This should comprise about 3% or so of your overall budget.

Conversely, the reception should comprise about 48% or so of your overall budget, as those who may not attend the wedding may attend the reception. Plus, you'll be at the reception longer and will be eating, drinking, dancing, etc. For that reason, you should consider such expenses as the cost of the cake, food, drinks, rentals, favors, and the reception site itself.

The attire and photography will take up a decent chunk of your wedding budget, usually in the neighborhood of 10-12%. Attire expenses include the bride's dress, shoes, undergarments and hosiery, hair, makeup, and jewelry.

For the groom, expenses will include his tuxedo or suit, bow tie, suspenders, studs, and cuff links. Photography expenses include the fees of the photographer and/or videographer, the albums, additional prints, and any disposable cameras.

The music expenses usually add up to about 8% of a typical wedding budget, due to the fact that you need to hire a band or DJ, cocktail hour musicians, and/or a sound system rental. Being that bands and DJ's need to be booked months in advance, the cost is usually a moderate to high amount and often non-refundable after a certain date.

The flowers normally cost about 8% of a typical wedding budget as well. These expenses usually include the bouquets for the bride and for the mother of the bride, as well as the maid-of-honor and bridesmaids'. They also include the flowers used during the ceremony, the flower-girl basket, and any corsages and centerpieces.

Of course, a wedding doesn't occur without the rings, usually costing about 3% of a typical wedding budget. Add in about 3% for the gifts, 3% for the stationery, and 2% for the transportation and you have all of the necessary elements needed to make a memorable wedding.

Therefore, utilize a wedding budget worksheet to keep track of everything that is needed for your wedding, makes sense. You want to have that worksheet when you are out and about around town or working on your computer, tablet, or Smartphone. You'll never know when you can make progress on an element or two for your wedding. By keeping track of everything, you'll not only remember to include everything that is needed, but be able to plan ahead and get it for the lowest price possible. Good luck!

CHAPTER 5: CHOOSING YOUR WEDDING PARTY?

Deciding who should be in your wedding party is not the easiest choice to make. Chances are, you likely have many people who would love to be in it, but there can be only one Maid of Honor and just a handful of bridesmaids.

Likewise, there can only be one Best Man and a few groomsmen, so there are only a handful of spots available. Odds are that you have more than that number of friends, even close friends. The information below should help you to choose the best people possible to include in your wedding party.

When choosing your Maid of Honor, a sister is usually the first choice. If you do not have a sister or have a sister you are close to, your very best friend is the next best option. Consider the person who has always stood by you, even in the toughest of times, and has told you things you didn't want to hear, even when it was good for you to hear them. This is the person who would probably best fit the role of your Maid of Honor.

Also consider that the person is responsible, as she will plan the bridal shower and the bachelorette party. In addition, she will be in charge of keeping the bridesmaids' fittings in good running order, as well as any other tasks that the bride has designated. The Maid of Honor may also be asked to give a toast at the reception.

The Best Man should probably be a brother of the groom, unless the groom doesn't have a brother or a brother he is close to. In that case, it should be a best friend who is responsible (i.e. he shouldn't drink too much.) In some parts of the United States, it is customary for the groom to choose his father to be Best Man. No matter who is chosen, it's best if the Best Man gets along well with the bride.

The Best Man is expected to organize all bachelor events and provide support to the groom in whatever way is needed. This includes keeping track of the wedding rings, especially if a young ring bearer is involved. The Best Man also is expected to make a toast at the reception.

Bridesmaids should be those who have a close relationship with the bride. These should include sisters, close cousins, and close friends. Including your fiancé's sister or sisters should also be considered.

These women will participate in all pre-wedding events, run errands, attend any tasting and site visits, and stay until the end of the reception. If they are not available for every party, that's acceptable, though they must send gifts for the bridal shower.

Groomsmen should be brothers, close cousins, and close friends of the groom. Additionally, the bride's brother or brothers should also be considered and included where possible. These men should help to seat guests, help the Best Man throw the bachelor party, and dance with the bridesmaids.

You should also carefully consider who the Flower Girl and Ring Bearer will be. The Flower Girl should likely be a cousin, a niece, a godchild, or a stepchild who is between the ages of three to six years old. This is not the same as junior bridesmaids, who are older and wear tween versions of the bridesmaids' dresses.

The Ring Bearer should be a young boy who can handle the responsibility of taking care of the rings (with help from an adult). The Ring Bearer should walk down the aisle with the Flower Girl.

Carefully considering who should be in your wedding party will help to ensure that the day is a memorable one for you and all involved. The people involved should be people who you are close to, who can perform the expected responsibilities, and who should be able to get along with the others in the wedding party. By carefully considering the people you are close to, choosing an appropriate wedding party shouldn't be too difficult or stressful.

CHAPTER 6: THE GUEST LIST

As you are planning for your upcoming wedding, you know that many important decisions have to be made, and they have to be made fairly quickly, especially when it comes to the venues, the catering, etc. Such decisions have to be made with a specific number of people in mind, namely the number of people coming to your wedding. Thus, you need to know who is on the guest list for coming to your wedding, and who will be left off.

Unfortunately, it's not an easy task to decide who will be invited to your wedding and who will be passed over. We will discuss how to formulate your guest list below.

First, you have to determine whether your parents are helping to cover the cost of your wedding. If so, then it would be appropriate to give them a few extra spots on the guest list for people they want to invite, even if they aren't your first choice. Your parents will appreciate it.

Second, you should evaluate all of your relationships with your friends and family and see who you have stayed in regular contact with. A common rule of thumb is, if you haven't been in regular contact with them for over a year, you can usually drop them from getting an invite.

Also consider whether business acquaintances and colleagues expect to attend your wedding or if you can remove them from the list. If they know that you are only planning to invite close family and friends, they will likely not be offended or disappointed that you did not invite them to your wedding.

You should talk with your significant other about any people in either of your families, or friends that you really do not want to attend your wedding. Exes that you've dated are people who you usually do not want to invite, for obvious reasons. Even if the ex is a good friend, it can be very touchy to invite that person to your wedding, so it is often best not to invite him or her.

If your parents want to invite someone you really don't want to have at your wedding, discuss it with them to see if you can come up with a compromise. You don't want to get into an argument with your parents if you can avoid it, as this is supposed to be a happy time for you and your family.

With that said, if someone who will make you uncomfortable is going to be invited to the wedding, work to either keep that person from coming or to resolve the awkward situation so it's still a happy time for all.

As you can see, creating the best wedding invite guest list is anything but easy. You have to consider your and your fiancé's families and friends, as well as your parents' wishes (especially if they are helping to pay for your wedding).

You have to carefully evaluate how close you are to the people you are considering inviting. Remember if it's been over a year since you've been in contact with them, you can usually leave them off of the list. The same usually holds true for colleagues and business acquaintances, especially if you just plan to invite close family and friends. By carefully considering the information above, you can more easily come up with the best guest list possible to make your wedding day the most special day possible.

Chapter 7: Choosing the Perfect Location for Your Wedding and Reception

Next on your agenda is finding and booking your perfect wedding venue. There are two parts to that with the first being to decide where you are going to get married. In a church, at a local park, in your own garden, at the beach, in the mountains, etc.? Then you need to decide where to hold your wedding reception.

It is so important to really think about both of these venues and plan carefully to ensure that your special day turns out in the way you want it. You must carefully consider where you will hold your wedding reception.

Your wedding reception is where family and friends gather after you have married to celebrate via food, drink, dancing, and music. This place has to have enough room to comfortably accommodate everyone. After all, this is supposed to be a social, enjoyable, fun atmosphere, and that can't happen if everyone is squeezed tightly into a small space or can't fit into the venue.

Therefore, you have several factors to think about ahead of time. You must consider how many guests you will be hosting. Obviously, if you have a very large party coming to your reception, all small- and most medium-sized locations will automatically be ruled out from the start. Of course, you don't want to rent out a space that is so large your small party doesn't feel the fun atmosphere. The size of the venue must be appropriate to the number of guests you will be inviting.

Another factor to take into consideration is how much you have in your budget. You certainly want to make your wedding day memorable with the perfect setting. But you certainly don't want to go over budget and put an undue and unnecessary strain on your new relationship right from the beginning.

If there is a venue that really catches your eye, but is out of your price range and budget, ask the vendors whether they offer special discounting for offseason weddings. Many vendors are happy to offer a discount in return for you committing to having your wedding there during their offseason.

Be sure when you are negotiating the price for having your wedding at a venue that you are certain on what you are getting. Vendors will vary on what they offer, such as tables, chairs, fully-functioning bar, etc. Some vendors include that in their stated prices, while others charge extra, so know what you're getting before you commit.

Be sure to think of your guests when you are choosing your wedding venue. After all, you don't want them to have to walk a mile to use a restroom if you are having an outdoor wedding. Or make it difficult for them to get from their vehicle to the place where you'll make your vows. Also, if small children will be there, consider whether there is ample room in case their parents need to take them elsewhere for a while to calm them down.

As you can see, choosing the right wedding venue can be quite challenging, as there are many factors you must consider, both for the two of you and for your guests.

You certainly don't want to have a venue that is too small or too large for your expected number of guests. While you want your wedding day to be memorable, that doesn't mean you have to overspend to make that happen. Keep the information above in mind as you plan your wedding day, and chances are, it will be the very special day you've always dreamt it would be.

Chapter 8: Planning Your Wedding Reception

While the wedding itself is the most important event of the day, the wedding reception is a close second. This is where you as the new couple, along with all of those who attended the wedding and perhaps a few more guests will go to celebrate the wedding.

The reception will be less formal and more of a chance to let "your hair hang down," relax, and have fun. Below, we will explore how to plan the reception so that a good time is had by all, including you.

Always keep in mind the reason behind the reception. It's likely that not everything is going to go according to plan, and that's okay. Don't let that ruin your evening. This reception is to be the start of your life journey together in holy matrimony, so don't let an unforeseen problem put a damper on this evening or on your marriage. You should let any problems that crop up to not ruin the mood and atmosphere of this evening.

Be sure to keep your guests in mind; you want to be confident that they are enjoying themselves as well. Most of your guests will probably have spent a good amount of money and time to be here. So you want to make sure that they are finding the atmosphere and event worthwhile. The reception should reflect your personality, including your humor, tastes, and preferences, so as to remind guests what makes you, you.

Decide on a specific style or theme you want your reception to have. This will also help you to determine where you will hold the reception.

Do you want the reception to be a large gathering or a smaller, more intimate group?

Do you want the reception to be more formal or informal? This also includes whether you want the meal to be fancy or more casual.

The theme or style can be based upon your favorite color(s) or something that is more complex, such as a specific time period that appeals to the two of you, a specific genre of music, or your favorite season.

Be sure to set your budget ahead of time so you can include and eliminate sites right away. This will help you move closer to your ideal site more quickly. Be sure to take into account the money that will be needed for decorations and centerpieces, food and beverages, music, the wedding cake, and the site itself.

Try to narrow down your ideal site to eight to nine sites right away. You can then call each one to see if they have availability on your wedding date. This can help to narrow down the choices even more.

You can then see if they have all the facilities and room necessary to accommodate your party. Then, you can schedule appointments to visit the venue to get a better idea if this will fit your dream reception or not. Be sure to have your list of questions handy so that you can truly determine which sites will make the final cut before deciding upon which site will be the one.

Choosing the proper wedding reception venue and having the best theme or style will take some planning ahead of time. You want to have the right theme or style that reflects your personality. You also want to be sure that your guests enjoy their time at your reception, as most will spend considerable amounts of time and money to attend.

By taking the information above into consideration, you will determine a venue and theme that will commemorate your relationship and be a fun, memorable time for all who attend.

Chapter 9: Organizing the Wedding Ceremony

To ensure that your wedding day is the best it can be, it's important to ensure that you include all of the important elements in a timely fashion. This means that you need to have at least a basic list and schedule of events, often known as a "wedding ceremony order." While there is no standard wedding ceremony order, there are elements that need to be present. We will go over what is needed and optional ones below.

First, determine whether you want your attendees to sign the wedding certificate or marriage license. This is not that common anymore, but it is an option to consider, especially if you have a small, more intimate wedding. Consider whether you want literature, love poetry, or religious wedding readings to be read during the early part of the ceremony.

The wedding processional is the entrance of the groom, the wedding party, and the bride. Determine what romantic ceremony music is to be playing, especially when the bride starts walking in. Do you want to have more of a traditional flavor, such as "Here Comes The Bride," or do you want more contemporary music such as the Coles' "Unforgettable"?

Decide upon how you will exchange your wedding rings. Will you state standard wedding vows, or will you write and state your own specific vows?

If you plan on stating your own specific vows, decide on whether you want to go over them together before the big day. This is especially true if you come from different faiths, as you may want to incorporate different religious references in your vows and want to be sure you are unified in your vows ahead of time.

Decide upon how the ceremony will be recognized. Will there be a community commitment to support the marriage or an officiate (priest, rabbi, etc.) present to officially recognize it and bless the marriage?

After this recognition and declaration of the marriage, the couple usually seals their first kiss as husband and wife. They then leave down the center aisle. After a period of time, the attendees will leave.

There may be pictures taken outside as the bride and groom will enter a limousine, a horse carriage, or some other form of transportation to be taken to the reception hall where the reception will take place. There is usually a "Just Married" sign on the back of the vehicle.

For a wedding to have the special meaning it is intended to, it is important to set up a program of all of the elements that you want included in it and in the proper order. You want to decide upon the opening readings and/or music, as well as the music for the entrance of the wedding party.

Particular attention for the entrance of the bride should be given, especially in regards to whether you should have traditional or contemporary music. Decide upon whether you will state standard vows or create more personalized ones. Decide whether an official will preside over the ceremony or if it will be more community-based.

All of these elements should be considered in order to ensure that your wedding ceremony will be as memorable as it should be for you and for all who attend.

Chapter 10: Choosing Your Wedding Music

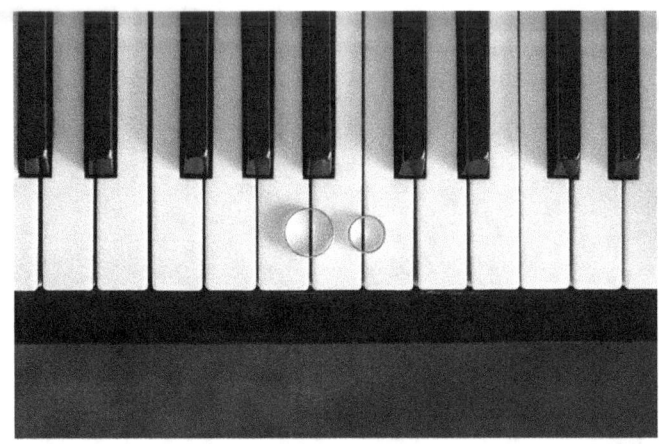

As you prepare for your upcoming wedding, many elements need to come together. This includes the venue, the catering, the flowers, and the music. Yes, you have to decide upon the music for your wedding. Choosing the right music is vital to creating the perfect atmosphere for your big day. In the section below, we will explore the factors you should consider when choosing your wedding music.

The music you select should really reflect your personality, your feelings, and your wedding theme. Your wedding day should be remembered for being a consistent theme of your love for each other. Plus, your love for all of the people who are invited to your wedding.

If your wedding has a strong central theme to it (such as a specific nationality or scene), then your music should complement that, and not be in contrast to it.

When it comes to your first dance, select a song with a tempo that is the perfect speed for both of you. You want to make sure to dance well and comfortably to the music, not look out-of-rhythm and uncomfortable. Additionally, always choose a song that has meaning to you both; it doesn't matter if the song is not trendy or popular. After all, this is your wedding, your day, so be sure that the song speaks to both of your hearts.

It helps if you think of your wedding as a movie with a plotline; this can help you to decide upon the music during the entire day. This includes the music during the actual wedding ceremony, the father-daughter dance, the bouquet or garter toss, etc.

Those pieces should be especially meaningful as compared to the background music that would play during the reception meal and other more casual moments. If you want to make some of your guests really feel special, you could have a song or two that really resonates with them during the day.

Be sure to coordinate with the band, DJ, or music group about the music lineup. You want to make sure you know what song is being played during which moments. After all, you don't want to get caught off-guard or not know what to do during a song because you weren't expecting it.

If you are having trouble coming up with good wedding songs, there are many online sites that can give you good options. Some, like OurWeddingSongs.com, will even provide ratings from people to give you an idea of what is popular and what isn't. While you want to have songs that resonate with you, you also want some that will be hits for your guests so that they will enjoy themselves too.

Selecting wedding music does require some thought and planning to ensure it matches up well with your wedding day. This day is meant to be one of the most important and enjoyable of your lives, so really spend some time to consider what songs you want to play and when you want them to be played during your day.

Remember that some popular love songs are about tragedy so listen to the lyrics first, before deciding if the song is appropriate for your wedding day.

Utilize the information above to help you come up with the best songs that will resonate with you and your guests to round out this special day.

Chapter 11: Selecting Wedding Invitations

As you prepare for your upcoming wedding, there are many elements you must carefully consider to ensure your wedding goes smoothly. Of course, you have to let people know that you are getting married and that they are cordially invited to attend. That means having wedding invitations. How do you go about getting those in a way that will fit your wedding style?

There are five main ways to get your wedding invitations made:

- Via a local stationery designer
- At a stationery store
- Via an online order
- Hiring a graphic designer
- Creating your own

Getting your wedding invitations done via a local stationery designer is a good choice if you want a high degree of customization and personalization that reflects your personality, life, journey, etc. You will often be able to work with the designer directly, and sometimes, even the printer too. So, if you plan to have several drafts before the final version is completed, this option is likely your best one.

Do expect to pay more for this option, as well as expect the order to take longer to complete since most local stationery designer are smaller operations with fewer resources.

Utilizing a stationery store will enable you to have many options of predesigned styles from a large range of known designers. You'll be able to look through many samples and catalogs put out by these designers to help you determine what will fit your wedding best.

You won't be able to do as much customization with this option, but you're bound to find something amongst all of the pre-designs that will fit your wedding theme and style. Employees will be able to adjust the wording and add some customized elements like monograms or maps. The pricing will be more competitive here than with local stationery designers.

As you might expect, online ordering your wedding invitations is becoming more popular. You can experiment with many different styles, layouts, colors, and more right on your computer screen.

Some online stores will even enable you to input all of your information and present a preview of what your wedding invitations will look like. Other online stores can mail you a physical proof within twenty-four hours so that you can see and feel it first-hand.

You can often obtain samples of styles and paper types for a small fee (that is usually credited towards your final order) to help avoid any last-minute bad surprises. The most competitive pricing is found here with this option.

Hiring a graphic designer will enable you to gain a unique design based on your wedding style and theme. Do note that this option will take a while, so it is best to look early (eight months or more) if this is the route you plan on taking. Besides this process being time-consuming, it is also costly, as you have to hire both the graphic designer and the printer.

Creating your own wedding invitations can be a great option for those looking to create something that is more distinctive. Plus it also helps to save on costs as well. Most craft stores have "do-it-yourself" kit, known as "printables." The design is there and the paper is pre-cut; all you need to do is input your details and print them out via a computer.

Some online designers will also provide this option to purchase designs and print them out. Do note that the selection is much more limited than with a stationery store, and it will take some time to print out all of the invitations based upon how many people are coming to your wedding.

As you can see, you have many viable options to obtain your wedding invitations. You just have to determine how distinctive you want them, how much you want to allocate from your budget toward them, and how much time you want to put into making them. By determining these factors and using the information above, you can decide upon the best choice to obtain your wedding invitations.

Chapter 12: Choosing Flowers for Your Wedding Day

As with any wedding, flowers help to make the occasion, whether it's part of the scene or where the flower girl is dropping them in the aisle. However, knowing what flowers to use for your wedding may not be the easiest thing to know. The information below will look into what you should consider before deciding upon what flowers to use in your wedding.

You should be deciding with your florist what flowers will work best at your wedding. You should give them as much information as possible to help you come upon your best choice. Describe what the overall theme of your wedding will be. Additionally, describe the dress you are to wear and provide pictures of the design if possible. If you are going to have flowers on your dress, make sure that these flowers will last for a while, as well as not be oozing liquid onto your dress.

You should also take into consideration whether the flowers you have in mind are currently in season or not. Obviously, if they are in season, it will cost less to obtain them than if they are not (provided you can even get them to begin with).

Also, take into consideration your guests. Do any of them suffer from allergies? If so, having the wrong type of flower as your main floral design is going to cause misery for him/her/them, so try to pick a flower that won't cause anyone to have a horrible experience at your wedding.

You should consider whether you plan on having the same flowers for your bridesmaids or if you will have different flowers. Again, you should consider the aforementioned factors of whether they are in season or if anyone is allergic to them before having your bridesmaids wear them. Of course, those flowers should go well with your flowers when you assemble together at your wedding.

The bridesmaids' bouquets should accentuate the bride, not detract from her. Thus, they are usually smaller than the bride's bouquet and can be a variation or contrast to her bouquet. The bouquets can also be used as flower arrangements at the reception, especially at the cake tables.

The groom's and family members' lapel pins will usually complement the wedding flowers. To really have the family stand out and be recognized, you could have a slight variation that identifies the family members from the other guests.

Keep in mind that table arrangements don't always need to have the wedding flowers present. Instead, you could use cheaper options, including ivy. Done in a decorative way, ivy can look just as spectacular for your table centerpieces. Or you could just sprinkle rose petals around the table settings.

As you can see, there are many decisions to make when it comes to your wedding flowers. You have to determine what is in season when your wedding takes place, if there are any attendees who are allergic to specific flowers, and what flowers go well with the bride's and bridesmaids' dresses.

By carefully considering the information above and working with your florist, you'll find the perfect flower(s) to go well with your wedding theme and not break the bank in the process.

Chapter 13: Your Wedding Pictures – Hire A Professional

As with many important events in your life, your wedding day and the reception are moments you want to capture in their glory. This means you want to hire a professional wedding photographer to capture those moments. This is in addition to any that you or your guests might take with your Smartphone's or cameras.

After all, you and your family will want to look back upon this day many years from now in a photo album book and/or on disc. Thus, it's vital you pick the best professional wedding photographer to capture those moments. We will explore how to choose the best professional wedding photographer below.

When you are interviewing prospective candidates, ask if they have photos of entire weddings available for viewing. This will give you a better idea of how they capture moments during a wedding. This allows you to see if they will capture the moments that you want to remember forever. You'll also see how good they are at the finite details that can make those pictures memorable. If possible, ask to see the raw prints themselves before they were retouched; this will give you a more accurate indication of how good and detailed the photographer is.

Ask for references that you can get into contact with. You want to speak with two or three former brides who have hired this photographer. Ask them if they would recommend this photographer to their best friends, and if so, why they would.

Ask if the photographer was punctual, was appropriately dressed, and if he/she was cordial throughout the entire process. Ask if their guests provided any comments on how good the pictures looked, etc.

Ask the photographer if you'll receive negatives or if the digital photos will be posted online. Negatives will take longer to receive, while digital photos will be up shortly after the wedding itself. This means that digital photos can be shared more quickly with family and friends. Be sure to know how long those photos will be up so that you can have them in your possession and let your family members and friends know so that they can have their own copies.

Confirm that the photographer you are interviewing is the one who will actually be working at your wedding. If he or she is part of a large company, that company may send another photographer out on the day of your wedding. Each photographer has their own style and skill when it comes to photo-taking. So it's important to ensure you know who the photographer will be on the day of your wedding. Most studios won't know who the actual photographer will be until that very day, but if they can't guarantee your first or second choice, you should consider moving onto a studio who can provide that guarantee.

Also check and confirm roughly how many pictures the photographer will take and how many images you will have to choose from. Know that some photographers will charge by roll of film, so be sure to recognize this ahead of time, and consider that when evaluating photographers, especially if you are on a tight budget.

Having the right wedding photographer can make all of the difference between having great photos to look back upon and having so-so or even poor photos. Certainly, you want to have the best photos possible, as you'll be looking back upon them years from now as you reminiscence with family and friends. Doing your due diligence now will ensure that you have the best wedding photos possible to capture the best moments from your special day.

Chapter 14: Wedding Cake Options

Another important element which goes into a wedding, is deciding upon what cake you are going to have. There are four main options to choose from, and we will go over each of these options below.

The first option is the one that most people are familiar with: Traditional and formal. This option involves a usually all-white cake. There are usually flowers on the cake, often made of a sugar paste. They can be in the shape of gardenias, calla lilies, and roses. These cakes normally are three to four inches high, each level being a tier. Each tier has four layers of cake in it. A common flavor combination used is a citrus-vanilla flavored cake iced with a butter cream frosting.

The second option is a contemporary or modern original design. This type of cake is taller than the traditional type, as the tiers are four to six inches high. In addition, the contemporary cake often has more elaborate designs than the traditional cake, and these designs usually repeat on the sides or top. The flavors of these cakes are more bold than traditional cakes; the flavors can include hazelnut, red velvet, and hummingbird (a type of carrot cake with a hint of pineapple flavoring).

The third option is the romantic and nontraditional cake. This type of cake is more whimsical in design; it can be based on virtually anything, even the design of a wedding dress. This cake is usually not uniform; as a result, the tiers can be of varying heights. Thus, the structure of the cake is not in a uniform pattern, making its appearance much different from traditional and contemporary cakes.

The fourth option is the casual wedding cake. This type of cake is a creative alternative to the traditional, three-tiered wedding cake. These are often in the form of many different variations of pies. This option has a laid-back feel to it, plus shows a country flavor as well. Due to the many different flavor options available, everyone is bound to be pleased by one flavor or another.

As you can see, there are four main types of wedding cake of which you can choose for your wedding. The first main question you have to consider is whether you want a traditional wedding cake or another option. If you are open to having something other than a traditional wedding cake, then you have several different options to choose from.

The second main question is how much you are willing to spend, as more ornate designs (such as those found in contemporary cakes) will cost more.

The third main question is how much of your personality and style do you want reflected in your cake? A traditional cake doesn't leave much room for personal design, whereas the other three do (especially the nontraditional option).

By carefully considering these questions and determining how much you want to spend, you will come up with a great cake that accentuates your wedding day that much more.

Chapter 15: Wedding Toasts and Etiquette

As part of the big day, a wedding speech is one of the most important aspects. It is usually done as a celebration of the happy couple, as well as to provide best wishes for a long and happy life together. The person who gives this may vary; it could be the father of the bride, a close friend, the best man, and/or the groom himself. We will look upon all of these situations below to help each person come up with a great wedding speech.

If a close friend is asked to provide a wedding speech, he or she may be a bit nervous. After all, it is a great honor to be asked to give such a wedding speech. This person knows that they want to give a great speech to honor the couple and commemorate this special occasion. They should think about all of the happy times they have shared with the couple, as well as what they know about the couple.

Based on these experiences and knowledge, the person should be able to come up with a speech. Their speech will be from the heart and will honor the happy couple. It will help to strengthen the relationship between them and between the friend and them.

If the father of the bride is asked to give a speech, it often follows a traditional formula. He will talk about his daughter, how his son-in-law cares for his daughter and how the family welcomes the son-in-law and his family into their family. He will also offer his best wishes for the new couple as they continue on their life journey together. The speech doesn't have to be formal, but it should stay within a three- to five-minute span, as there will be other speeches to follow.

The groom's speech will normally follow the father of the bride as a type of "answer" to his speech. The groom's speech should thank the bride's family and the guests. It should especially thank those (including the bride's family) for helping to make the wedding possible, though money and finances should never be mentioned directly. The groom can make mention of one or two special people who were always there to help out and what that person or those people mean to himself and his new wife.

In some weddings, the bride will also speak. If this is the case, then be sure that the groom and bride split up the thanks and stories to be shared. Essentially, they would be two halves of the speech. Combined, they should be about three to five minutes, about the same time as the father of the bride's speech. Usually, the groom's speech will end with a toast to his new family, so it makes sense for the bride to speak first, then the groom, if both are going to speak.

The best man's speech is often the last speech to be made. If the maid of honor is going to speak, then she should speak first, followed by the best man.

Both of them are representations of all of the people who are there to attend the wedding. Combined with the fact that this speech is often the last one, it is usually less formal than the other speeches. One of the best strategies is to tell a short story about the couple, something that is humorous. Be sure that it's a fun story rather than an embarrassing one, as the couple should be honored.

The best man and maid of honor should thank the bride and groom for choosing them to serve in those roles and offer a toast. They can also thank the guests by toasting them for helping to make the event a memorable one.

Chapter 16: Choosing Your Honeymoon Destination

Besides planning for the wedding and reception, it's important to plan your honeymoon destination. Some couples will hold off on a honeymoon until later due to their career commitments or financial reasons. Many will take their honeymoon shortly after their wedding to help bring them closer together before they return to their daily routines.

Presuming you plan on having a honeymoon right after you get married, the following information should prove helpful to come up with the best honeymoon destination without breaking your budget.

First, make a budget ahead of time. Determine how much money you plan on spending on your honeymoon. This will help you to determine which options are realistically available to you to choose from.

Determine whether you want to use a travel agent or not. Travel agents can help to take much of the busywork out of planning your honeymoon. Not all travel agents are expensive so it may be a worthwhile option. This can be especially helpful if planning for your wedding and reception are taking considerable amounts of time and attention.

Determine where you want to go on your honeymoon. Your future spouse and you may have different ideas on what would constitute the perfect honeymoon. Discuss your ideas with each other to come up with a destination that will fit in well with both of your ideas for a memorable honeymoon. Also take into consideration the time of year and what the weather will be like to increase the chances you can do the activities you want to do, especially if they are outdoor activities.

Buy the plane tickets to get there. If you are using frequent flier miles, be certain to book as early as eleven months ahead of time. This will increase your chances of obtaining a nonstop flight as well. Be sure to reserve your hotel early and this is especially the case for European locations, as many of their hotels are smaller.

When you get closer to the time of your honeymoon, about six months out, book transportation, such as a rental car or train tickets. If you are heading to Europe and need to utilize Eurail, the main European train network, get the overall pass now, then schedule seats about sixty or so dates out when the updated schedules are released.

Schedule any dinner reservations and get any visas or other documentation if needed, well ahead of time. This includes getting or renewing your passport. It is also wise to purchase travel insurance in the event your trip gets canceled due to a natural event (such as a hurricane). Find out if you require any vaccinations, and schedule an appointment with your doctor. If you are headed to an exotic location you may need certain shots. You certainly want to avoid any illnesses during your honeymoon or after you've returned from it.

Planning your honeymoon ahead of time is vital. This allows you to have that memorable honeymoon you want to have after your wedding, and before you return to your daily routines involving your careers and responsibilities.

Be sure you agree upon a site that will fulfill both of your visions for a dream honeymoon. Take steps to arrange the flight, the hotel reservations, passports, visas, and vaccinations (if needed), dinner reservations, and travel insurance. By preparing ahead of time, you can ensure that your honeymoon will be a memorable start for the two of you.

CHAPTER 17: WEDDING TO-DO LIST

Here's a quick recap of all the major things you need to plan in advance.

- Wedding Budget
- Wedding Party
- Guest List
- Ceremony Location
- Reception Location
- Invitations
- Flowers
- Cake
- Wedding Dress
- Bridesmaid Dresses
- Photographer
- Music
- Honeymoon

You will have a ton of other items that will need to be found, reserved, picked up, checked on, etc. before and during your wedding. It never hurts to delegate some items to people whom you trust. Choose a family member or close friend that you have complete trust and faith in to reduce your stress and anxiety.

MEET THE AUTHOR

April Hall came to wedding planning naturally as she was fascinated with weddings at a young age and preferred bridal and wedding magazines over age appropriate magazines such as Teen Beat and Seventeen. April will tell you she doesn't like to be called a planner or consultant. She prefers to be called a wedding producer because she takes a couple's dreams and produces the magical event that far surpasses merely planning or advising. April began planning weddings when she was still in college and applied for her first business license before she graduated. April's attention to detail and her dedication to her couples along with her exceptional customer service that embraces family and guests alike has made her services and reputation one of a kind and in demand.

April's undergraduate degree in Art and her MBA guarantee that she has the creative skills for beautiful dreams and the business skills to manage a budget and get a complex event produced on time. When April isn't creating fairy tale weddings, she enjoys spending her time with her husband, her two energetic sons and two equally energetic dogs.

WEDDING PLANNING FOR THE BRIDE-TO-BE

April Hall has been creating wedding magic for over 15 years as she grows and enhances her business and has developed customer relationships that have seen her produce multiple weddings from the same families. April Hall is a wedding producer extraordinaire!

www.ingramcontent.com/pod-product-compliance
Lightning Source LLC
LaVergne TN
LVHW021738060526
838200LV00052B/3349